CHILDREN'S ATLAS OF SCOTLAND

CHILDREN'S ATLAS OF SCOTLAND

Theodore Rowland-Entwistle

and

Clare Oliver

Miles Kelly
PUBLISHING

First published in 2000 by
Miles Kelly Publishing Ltd
Bardfield Centre, Great Bardfield, Essex, CM7 4SL

Copyright © 2000 Miles Kelly Publishing

2 4 6 8 10 9 7 5 3 1

Editor: Clare Oliver
Designer: Sally Boothroyd
Project Manager: Kate Miles
Art Director: Clare Sleven
Editorial Director: Paula Borton
Production: Rachel Jones
Artwork Commissioning: Susanne Grant, Lynne French, Natasha Smith
Picture Research: Janice Bracken, Lesley Cartlidge, Liberty Newton
Cartography: Digital Wisdom
Index: Lynn Bresler
Additonal help from Ian Paulyn & Jane Walker
Reproduction House: DPI

British Library Cataloguing-in-Publication Data
A catalogue record for this book is available from the British Library

ISBN 1-902947-53-3

Printed in Hong Kong

CAN YOU FIND?

Look out for these boxes as you
read this book. They suggest places
to look for on the regional maps.
Why not see if you can use the
lettered and numbered borders on
the map pages to work out map
co-ordinates for each place?
You can find out how to use map
co-ordinates on page 37.
And on page 39 you will find answers
for all the 'Can You Find?' locations,
written as co-ordinates.

MAP ICONS

Look out for the icons on the maps.
They show where there are special
features. They represent:

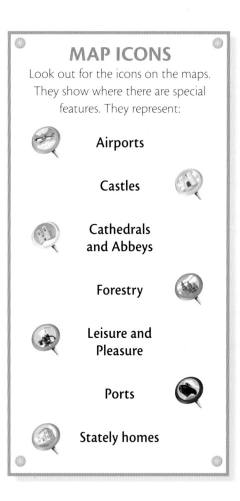

Airports

Castles

Cathedrals
and Abbeys

Forestry

Leisure and
Pleasure

Ports

Stately homes

Contents

About map icons & Can You Find?   4

Contents   5

SCOTLAND: INTRODUCTION   6

Scotland: Physical features   8

Edinburgh   10

Dumfries and Galloway   12

Borders   14

Lothian   16

Strathclyde   18

Central Scotland   22

Tayside and Fife   24

Grampian   26

Highland   28

The Western Isles   30

Orkney   32

Shetland   34

Glossary   36

Map Co-ordinates   37

Index   38

Can you find? answers   39

Acknowledgements   40

Scotland

SCOTLAND IS THE NORTHERNMOST PART of the island of Great Britain, making up about one-third of its total area. In addition to the mainland, Scotland has hundreds of offshore islands, which can be divided in three major groups: the Hebrides off the west coast, and the Orkney Islands and Shetland Islands to the north. Edinburgh is Scotland's capital city.

◄ Scottish thistle
In the 1400s James III of Scotland made the thistle his royal emblem. There is still an order of Scottish knights known as the Knights of the Thistle.

The earliest settlers arrived in Scotland about 8,000 years ago. When the Romans arrived in AD70, the inhabitants of Scotland living north of the river Clyde were mostly Picts, while British tribes lived in the border area. Later invaders were the Scots from Ireland, the Angles from Germany and the Vikings from Scandinavia.

Kenneth MacAlpin, a Scottish king, ruled the country in the AD800s. The first person to rule the whole country was Malcolm II, who came to the throne in 1005. Throughout the Middle Ages there were wars between Scotland and England. Edward I of England tried to conquer Scotland in the 1300s, but eventually Robert the Bruce secured Scotland's independence in 1328. The Stewarts, who were descended from Robert the Bruce's daughter Marjorie, ruled Scotland for the next 300 years.

Scotland became linked to England when the Stuart king, James VI of Scotland, succeeded the English queen, Elizabeth I, in 1603. In 1707 an Act of Union formally joined the two countries.

▲ River Tay
Scotland's earliest settlements were built near sources of fresh water.

▲ The Scottish Highlands
One of Scotland's chief landmarks is Ben Nevis, Britain's highest mountain. It rises to a height of 1,343 metres.

▼ Iron Age builders
The Picts were warlike people who settled northeastern Scotland. They lived in underground houses, known as weems, and built defensive round towers, known as brochs.

◄ Patron saint of Scotland
Andrew is Russia's patron saint as well as Scotland's. He was one of Christ's disciples. Like Christ, Andrew was crucified, which is why his symbol is a cross.

▲ Robert I of Scotland
Robert the Bruce was crowned king of Scotland in 1306. Almost at once he was on the run from the armies of Edward I, and later Edward II, of England. Robert finally defeated the English at Bannockburn in 1314.

Government of Scotland

Today Scotland is part of the United Kingdom of Great Britain and Northern Ireland. However, Scotland has its own legal, educational and local government systems. In 1999 the Scottish Parliament took control of many of Scotland's affairs for the first time in almost 300 years.

The Scottish Parliament

The Parliament, which consists of 129 MPs elected by the Scottish people, meets in Edinburgh. An executive consisting of a First Minister and other ministers is in charge. The Secretary of State for Scotland remains in the Cabinet of the UK government, and liaises with the First Minister. Foreign, defence, and economic matters are the responsibility of the Parliament at Westminster.

COUNTRY FACTS

SCOTLAND
Area: 78,789 sq km
Population: 5,128,000
Capital: Edinburgh
Major cities: Aberdeen, Dundee, Glasgow
Official language: English (Scottish Gaelic is spoken by 1.4 percent of the population)
Main religions: Church of Scotland (Presbyterian), Scottish Episcopal Church, Roman Catholicism
Currency: Pound sterling (£)
Highest point: Ben Nevis (1,343 m)
Longest river: Tay (188 km)
Largest lake: Loch Lomond (60 sq km)

▼ James VI's family tree
The Scottish king, James VI, traced his ancestry back more than two centuries to heroic Robert the Bruce.

▼ Church of Scotland
The Calvinist John Knox founded the Presbyterian Church of Scotland in the 1500s. This was a break away from the Roman Catholic Church. There is a statue of Knox in front of St Giles' Cathedral, Edinburgh, where he was dean.

Robert m Marjorie, Countess of Carrick

(1) Isobel of Mar m ROBERT I, the Bruce m (2) Elizabeth
1306–1329

(1) Joanna m DAVID II m (2) Margaret
1329–1371

Walter FitzAlan, m Marjory Bruce
6th High Steward of Scotland

(1) Elizabeth Mure m ROBERT II m (2) Euphemia Ross
1371–1390

ROBERT III m Annabella Drummond
1390–1406

JAMES I m Joan Beaufort
1406–1437

JAMES II m Mary of Gueldres
1437–1460

JAMES III m Margaret of Denmark
1460–1488

(1) JAMES IV m Margaret Tudor m (2) Archibald Douglas, m (3) Henry Stewart,
1488–1513 6th Earl of Angus Lord Methven

(1) Madeleine m JAMES V m (2) Mary of Guise
of France 1513–1542

Margaret Douglas m Matthew Stewart
13th Earl of Lennox

(1) Francis II m MARY, m (2) Henry Stewart, Lord Darnley m (3) James Hepburn, 4th Earl of Bothwell
King of QUEEN
France OF SCOTS
1542–1567

JAMES VI m Anne of Denmark
King of Scotland
1567–1625
King of England
1603–1625

(Dates show length of reign)

Scotland Physical features

SCOTLAND IS VERY DIFFERENT FROM ENGLAND. This is not surprising when you discover that, more than 400 million years ago, the two countries were on different continents. The two land masses collided, and it is possible to trace where they joined together deep under the border area of Scotland and England. Scotland's rugged mountains and scenery are the result of movements in the Earth's crust over millions of years.

Three geographical regions make up mainland Scotland. Bordering England are the Southern Uplands, which consist mostly of rolling moors with fertile soil. In the south, the Cheviot Hills form the border with England. Next come the Central Lowlands, through which three major rivers, the Clyde, the Forth and the Tay, flow. This area has the best farmland and mineral resources. The third region is the Highlands, which cover two-thirds of the country. This region is mountainous, with jagged peaks and numerous lakes, known as lochs. The most mountainous part is in the west. Most people in the Highland region live in the coastal lowlands, especially in the east.

▼ **The Scottish 'Alps'**
Winter snow on the Highland slopes provides good skiing opportunities at Aviemore.

▲ **Mountain landscape**
Scotland's mountains were shaped by glaciers, moving sheets of ice that covered the land during the last Ice Age.

▲ **Loch Duich**
Glaciers carved out hollows in the surface of the land. These have since filled with water to form the hundreds of lochs which are such a feature of the Highlands.

◀ **Shifting lands**
Once separated by sea, Scotland and England were pushed together as a result of continental drift. This was the movement of the Earth's land masses that took place over a period of millions of years:
1 Around 280 mya, the land formed one giant supercontinent, Pangaea
2 Around 180 mya, Pangaea split into Laurasia (to the north) and Gondwanaland (to the south)
3 Around 65 mya, the Atlantic Ocean widened
4 Today, the land masses are grouped into seven continents

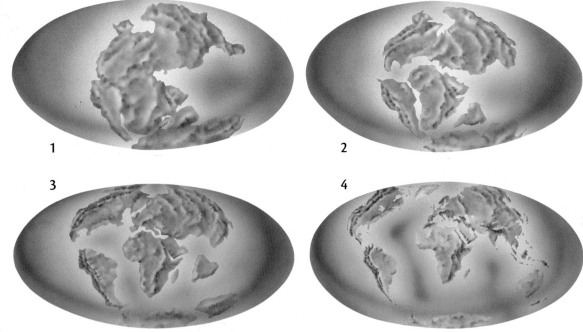

1

2

3

4

◀ Stormy seas
The rocky Grampian coast takes a regular battering from the North Sea waves.

ATLANTIC OCEAN

NORTH SEA

Moving mountains

When the Atlantic Ocean began to open up about sixty-five million years ago, the land which is now Scotland remained joined to what is now Europe. The rest of that continent formed what is now North America. The hard rocks that make up Scotland's mountains were crushed, folded and distorted many times – and even turned upside down! Originally the mountains were sharp and jagged. Millions of years of action by wind, rain and ice have worn them down, so they are much lower than their original height with rounded outlines.

◀ Highs and lows
The Scottish Lowlands are the best region for arable farming. In the Highlands, farmers raise sheep and a breed of hardy beef cattle, known as the Aberdeen Angus.

▲ Firth of Forth
The river Forth, with its long estuary, or firth, marks the dividing line between the Highlands and the rest of Scotland.

The Great Glen

Glen Mor, or the Great Glen, is the remains of a huge geological fault in the Earth's crust. It may once have been similar to the earthquake-prone San Andreas Fault in California, where two of the Earth's plates are grating against one another.

Edinburgh

EDINBURGH HAS BEEN THE CAPITAL OF SCOTLAND since the beginning of the 15th century, when it replaced the Scottish capital of Perth. In 1999 it became the seat of the revived Scottish Parliament. Built around the banks of the Forth Estuary, Edinburgh is ideally sited in the Central Lowlands, a region of rich farmland and extensive mineral deposits.

▲ **Unfinished business**
Funds to build the Greek-style National Monument, atop Calton Hill, ran out after just 12 columns were complete.

▼ **Royal guesthouse**
The Palace of Holyroodhouse is the Queen's official residence in Scotland.

Edinburgh has direct rail and road links with London, and air services link it with United Kingdom cities and several capital cities in continental Europe. Rail and road bridges span the Firth of Forth to link the city with the northern part of the country. There are many different industries in and around the capital, including brewing, whisky distilling, and textile and paper manufacturing. Edinburgh is also a key business centre, with many banks and insurance offices.

Important buildings

The magnificent castle, perched high up on its rocky crag, dominates the city. It stands on the plug of a long-dead volcano. To the north of the castle rock is a valley through which the railway line runs, and on the far side is Princes Street, one of the main shopping centres. Nearby is Calton Hill, another volcanic plug, which is topped by the Nelson Monument. To the east of the city is the magnificent hill of Arthur's Seat, set in Holyrood Park. On the edge of the park stands the Palace of Holyroodhouse. Several Scottish kings and queens are buried in the palace's vault. Other notable buildings include St Giles' Cathedral, the Royal Observatory on Calton Hill, and Register House.

▲ **Street juggler**
Edinburgh's International Festival of Music and Dance attracts hoards of tourists to the city each August. Performers include actors, comedians and street entertainers.

▼ **Museum of Scotland**
Opened in 1998, the new Museum of Scotland houses a collection of artefacts from Scottish history.

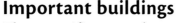

SCHOOL
TIMEKINS

PLACES OF INTEREST

ART GALLERIES
National Gallery of Scotland, Royal Scottish Academy, Scottish National Gallery of Modern Art, Scottish National Portrait Gallery

PARKS
Holyrood Park, Meadow Park, Princes Street Gardens, Ramsay Garden, Royal Terrace Gardens

PLACES OF WORSHIP
Canongate Kirk, Greyfriars Kirk, Highland Tolbooth Kirk, St Giles' Cathedral, St Mary's Episcopal Cathedral, Tron Kirk

MUSEUMS
Museum of Childhood, Museum of Scotland, The People's Story, Royal Museum of Scotland, Scotch Whisky Heritage Centre, The Writers' Museum

OTHER ATTRACTIONS
Abbey Lairds, Arthur's Seat, Camera Obscura, Edinburgh Castle, Edinburgh Experience, Flodden Wall, National Monument, Palace of Holyroodhouse, Royal Botanic Garden

The oldest of the city's three universities was founded in 1583. In addition, Edinburgh boasts two famous medical colleges: the Royal College of Physicians of Edinburgh and the Royal College of Surgeons of Edinburgh. The Meadowbank Sports Centre hosted the 1970 Commonwealth Games.

▲ **Edinburgh streets**
Many of Edinburgh's buildings date to the 1700s. The 37-km-long Water of Leith meanders through the city.

Moments in history

There has been a settlement at Edinburgh since 850BC. Edinburgh grew in the AD1000s when David I established his court at Edinburgh Castle. In 1513 the English defeated the Scots at the Battle of Flodden, killing James IV and 10,000 of his men. Remains of Flodden Wall can still be seen on the High Street. When James VI became king of England in 1603, the royal court moved to London. In the 1700s many new buildings were erected to the north of the old city. In the 1800s the population of the city quadrupled, and many terraced houses were built. Today, the city has a population of 420,170.

◀ **Regimental entertainment**
Against the impressive backdrop of the castle, Edinburgh's Military Tattoo is held at the end of August each year, to coincide with the Edinburgh Festival.

◀ **Wall plaque, the Royal Mile**
Leading up to Edinburgh Castle, the Royal Mile is lined with beautiful buildings, some dating to the 1400s.

▲ **Seat of learning**
Students of Edinburgh University have included Charles Darwin, writers Thomas Carlyle and Sir Walter Scott, and the inventor Alexander Graham Bell.

Dumfries and Galloway

▼ Poem in stone
Ruthwell Cross dates from the AD700s. It is covered with ancient runes, or writing. The inscription includes part of an Old English poem called *The Dream of the Rood*, which is about Christ's crucifixion.

▼ Religious ruins
Sweetheart Abbey, near Kirkcudbright, was a centre for Cistercian monks from 1273 until 1603.

THE DUMFRIES AND GALLOWAY REGION lies in southwestern Scotland. It contains the former counties of Dumfriesshire, Kirkcudbrightshire and Wigtownshire. Ireland is only a few kilometres away across a stretch of water called the North Channel.

Most of this region is low-lying coastal land, broken up by rocky headlands. To the north lies a plateau of moorland. In the west is a hammer-head shaped peninsula called the Rhins of Galloway. It stretches south to the Mull of Galloway, a towering 64-metre-high cliff. In the northern part of the Rhins is the port of Stranraer, which runs a regular shipping service to Larne in Northern Ireland.

◄ Rose-tinted fortress
Caerlaverock Castle has stood on the shores of the Solway Firth since the 1290s. It was built from unusual, pinkish-coloured stone.

Farming and industry

Farmers in Dumfries and Galloway rear sheep, cattle and pigs, and grow oats, turnips and other cattle feed. Potatoes are the main crop grown for human consumption. There are five hydroelectric power stations in Kirkcudbrightshire, which use water from local rivers and lochs to generate electricity. Wigtown is being developed as the centre of Scotland's book trade. Tourism is important in the region. Kirkcudbright attracts artists and anglers. The fishing is also good at Gatehouse of Fleet on the river Fleet.

▲ Barnacle goose

GRETNA GREEN
Close to the border with England lies the village of Gretna Green. For centuries English couples ran away and married here. Under Scots law, under-age brides did not need their parents' permission to marry.

◄ Salmon leap
Scotland is famous for its freshwater fish. Wild salmon head upriver each year to their spawning grounds.

► Power station
This hydroelectric dam harnesses water power. The energy of water driving a turbine is changed into electrical energy at the power station.

Moments in history

People have lived in this region since around 5000BC. The Stone Age tombs at Cairnholy, near Gatehouse of Fleet, date from about 3000BC. At Burnswark, near Lockerbie, you can see the remains of an Iron Age hill fort and two Roman camps. St Ninian, who founded a monastery at Whithorn, near Burrow Head, is said to have brought Christianity to the area during the 4th century. Later, Viking invaders from Scandinavia and Normans from England occupied the area. It became a Scottish shire, or county, in the 1400s.

▲ Viking invaders

COUNTY FACTS

DUMFRIES AND GALLOWAY
Area: 6,370 sq km
Population: 144,856
Administrative centre: Dumfries
Other towns: Kirkcudbright, Stranraer

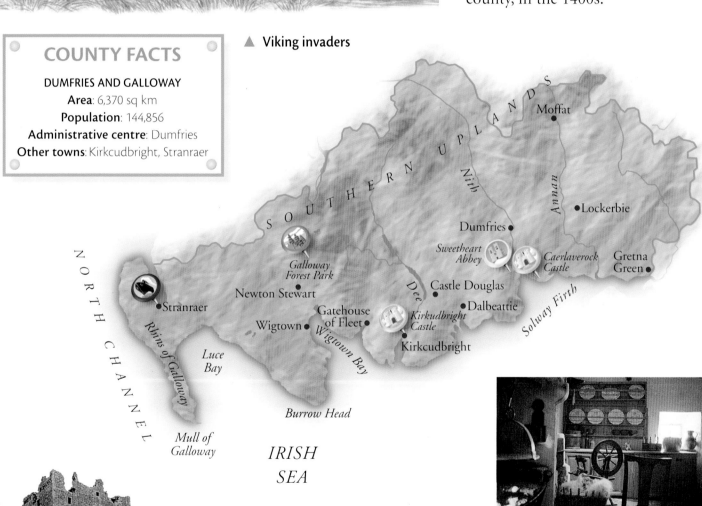

IRISH
SEA

◀ **Grim and grey**
Now in ruins, Threave Castle on the river Dee was the home of a fierce clan, the Black Douglases. The earls of Douglas found a grisly use for the post that sticks out above the castle doorway. This was where they hung 'tassels' – that is, their poor enemies!

ROBBIE'S HOUSE

Robert Burns was one of Scotland's greatest poets. He spent the last five years of his life in Dumfries, where he worked as a tax collector. He described the town as 'Maggie by the Banks o' Nith.' His house is now a museum.

Borders

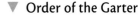

▼ Melrose Abbey

These Gothic ruins near Galashiels were restored by Sir Walter Scott in the 1800s. Robert the Bruce's heart is buried here.

▼ Order of the Garter

Coldstream, on the banks of the river Tweed, was the birthplace of the British Army's oldest regiment, the Coldstream Guards. The regiment's emblem is the Star of the Order of the Garter.

THE SCOTTISH BORDERS HAS A LONG FRONTIER with England, sloping from southwest to northeast. Much of the land on either side of the border is wild country, with steep hills, fast-flowing streams and few towns or villages. The Borders region replaced the historic counties of Berwickshire, Peeblesshire, Roxburghshire and Selkirkshire.

Most of the land in the Scottish Borders forms part of the Southern Uplands. These well-worn, rounded hills are covered with grass and heather. They include the Cheviots along the English border – the highest peak is The Cheviot (816 metres). To the north are the Pentland, Moorfoot and Lammermuir Hills. In the east is a lowland area called the Merse, a rich farming region. The river Tweed, with its many tributaries, flows between the hills and through the fertile Merse to the sea. The region has warm summers and cold winters. Its rainfall is very variable, ranging from 625 to 1,750 mm per year.

◀ Boats of Berwickshire

Eyemouth is the region's chief fishing harbour.

Farming and industry

About half of the land in the Borders is used for grazing sheep and cattle. Farmers grow barley, wheat and potatoes, and grass, turnips and other crops for animal feed. Ettrick Forest is the remains of a huge ancient forest, and there are modern plantations of pine. Foxes, badgers and rabbits are common, and roe-deer live in some of the forests. Salmon breed in the river Tweed. There is a small amount of industry, largely textiles, with tweed cloth as the main output. Jedburgh is a centre of the tweed industry.

◀ Scots pine

▶ Rabbit

▶ River Tweed

Moments in history

The Borders were part of the English kingdom of Northumbria until the early AD1000s, when the region was taken into Scotland. An exception was the town of Berwick-upon-Tweed, which changed hands between England and Scotland several times before finally becoming part of England in 1482. At the same time, powerful Scottish families, such as the Douglases, competed with one another for power. Greenknowe Tower, near Earlston, was built as a stronghold in 1581, when border skirmishes were still common.

▲ **Greedy reivers**
From the 1200s to the 1500s the whole area of the Borders was ravaged by wars, skirmishes and reiving (plundering).

NORTH SEA

COUNTY FACTS

BORDERS
Area: 4,675 sq km
Population: 105,300
Administrative centre: Melrose
Other cities: Duns, Jedburgh, Peebles, Selkirk

▶ **Duns Scotus**

WHAT'S IN A NAME?
The Franciscan priest and philosopher Duns Scotus was born at Duns in Berwickshire in 1265. The word 'dunce' comes from his name, because his followers were supposed to be against learning.

▲ **Romantic house**
Abbotsford is a large house near Melrose. It was built by the novelist and poet Sir Walter Scott, who wrote his 30 'Waverley novels' there. These were romantic tales of knights and ladies, set in the Scottish Borders.

F
E
D
C
B
A

Lothian

Lothian has several doocots, or dovecots, where people bred rock doves (pigeons) for eggs and meat. This doocot at West Saltoun looks like a miniature, turreted castle!

▼ Firth of Forth

LOTHIAN IS MADE UP OF THE HISTORIC counties of West Lothian, Midlothian and East Lothian. The region makes up only about two percent of Scotland's total area, but almost 30 percent of the country's population live there, mostly in the city of Edinburgh.

Lothian, which forms part of the Central Lowlands of Scotland, is bordered by moorland hills. To the southwest are the Pentland Hills, the highest part of which is Scald Law (580 metres). To the southeast are the Moorfoot and Lammermuir Hills, many of which are long-extinct volcanoes. The highest point is Blackhope Scar (650 metres). Four main rivers drain the region – the Almond, the Tyne, the Esk and the Water of Leith.

Towns, transport and industry

Two huge bridges near Edinburgh, the Forth Rail Bridge and the Forth Road Bridge, link Lothian with the north bank of the river Forth. Besides Edinburgh, the region's largest towns are Livingston, Musselburgh, Bathgate, Whitburn, Penicuick and Dalkeith. In 1962 Livingston was a village with a population of only 2,000. It was designated as a 'new town' in that year, and by 1991 it had over 41,000 inhabitants. There are firms producing electronics and other technological products at Dalkeith and Livingston, but most of the region's industry is concentrated in Edinburgh.

▲ Seaweed

▼ Bass Rock
Just off the coast of East Lothian, this 107-metre-high rock is the plug of a long-extinct volcano.

▼ Circuit board
There are electronics companies in and around Dalkeith.

◀ Threshing grain
Andrew Meikle was a millwright at Houston Mill, near Dunbar. In 1788 he patented a brand-new threshing machine that removed wheat and grain from their husks, or chaff.

Farming and wildlife

Arable farming and market gardening are extensive in Lothian. Farmers raise sheep in the Lammermuir Hills, as well as cattle and chickens. Seabird colonies thrive on the Bass Rock, North Berwick Law and other islands in the Firth of Forth, and in a reserve at Aberlady Bay. The Isle of May, in the mouth of the Firth, is used as a stopover by small migrating birds, such as goldcrests, as well as by seabirds. Seals breed on the island, too.

▲ Goldcrest

EAST LOTHIAN
Area: 677 sq km
Population: 85,840
Administrative centre: Haddington

MIDLOTHIAN
Area: 356 sq km
Population: 79,910
Administrative centre: Dalkeith

WEST LOTHIAN
Area: 425 sq km
Population: 146,730
Administrative centre: Livingston

CITY OF EDINBURGH
Area: 262 sq km
Population: 420,170

NORTH SEA

Firth of Forth   Bass Rock

Edinburgh Airport   Edinburgh   Edinburgh Castle   North Berwick   Dunbar Castle   Dunbar

Almond   Water of Leith   PENTLAND HILLS   Esk   Tyne   MOORFOOT HILLS

F

E

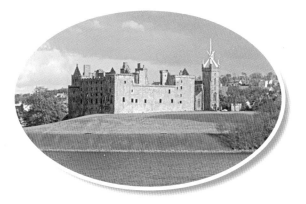

▲ **Roofless ruins**

Linlithgow Palace, where Mary, Queen of Scots was born in 1542, was a favourite residence of Scottish kings. West Lothian used to be called Linlithgowshire.

LOTHIAN'S CASTLES

The region has several notable castles besides Edinburgh Castle. In 1339 the Countess of March and Dunbar, known as Black Agnes, successfully defended Dunbar Castle against a siege. Hailes Castle was reduced to ruins by Oliver Cromwell during the English Civil War. Crichton Castle was begun in the 1400s and enlarged in the 1500s. Tantallon Castle, which was owned by the Douglas family, is a cliff-top stronghold that juts into the North Sea.

D

▼ **Black Agnes defends Dunbar**

C

BRILLIANT BRIDGE

The Forth Rail Bridge was completed in 1890 after seven years' work and the loss of 60 workers' lives. The bridge's intricate, iron girders take three years to repaint. Nearby is the Forth Road Suspension Bridge, completed in 1964.

B

A

4   3   2   1

Strathclyde

▼ **Isle of Mull**
The tiny settlement of Calgary is built on a small, secluded bay on the northwest corner of the island.

◀ **Peregrine falcon**

▼ **Sir Walter Scott**
Scott's statue looks out across the city of Glasgow from a 24-metre-high column in George Square.

THE KINGDOM OF STRATHCLYDE covered southwest Scotland and northwest England about 1,000 years ago. The name was revived in 1975 for the new region of Strathclyde. Modern Strathclyde, which is Scotland's most densely-populated region, is dominated by the city of Glasgow.

In the northwest of Strathclyde there are sea lochs, peninsulas and islands, including part of the Inner Hebrides and the islands of Arran and Mull. The rest of Strathclyde is hilly and includes parts of the Central Lowlands, the Highlands to the north and the Southern Uplands to the south. The river Clyde flows through the Central Lowlands in a great curve, stretching for 170 kilometres from the Lowther Hills to Dumbarton. The Firth of Clyde completes the horseshoe shape.

Water world

Many of the lochs of Argyll and Bute are sea lochs or inlets, such as the Gare Loch and Lochs Long, Fyne, Goil, Gilp, Craignish and Melfort. Loch Linnhe in the north is the start of the Great Glen that crosses the Highland Region. Of the landlocked lochs, the largest are Loch Lomond – which forms most of the boundary with Stirling – Loch Awe and Loch Etive. Fast-flowing streams from the mountains feed these lochs. The name Argyll comes from the Gaelic *Earraghaidheal* which means 'coastland of the Gael.'

Glasgow City

The Celtic for Glasgow, *Glas Ghu*, or the 'Green Glen,' refers to the valley where most of the city lies. The city straddles the river Clyde, with most business and industry on the north bank. Glasgow's heavy industries developed in the 1800s, but by the 1970s most had closed down. Today the city is a major trading and administrative centre. It has a university, an airport and good transport links to England, Edinburgh and the north of Scotland. Glasgow has a busy port and the banks of the Clyde are lined with docks, quays and shipyards.

◀ **Bottlenose dolphin**
The Isle of Mull is a good place for spotting marine mammals such as minke whales, bottlenose dolphins and seals.

Coll

Tiree

Staffa

Iona

Colon

▲ **Dunoon, Argyll**
This seaside resort is on the northwestern shore of the Firth of Clyde.

ATLANTIC OCEAN

Port Eller

▼ **Fingal's Cave**
This amazing cave on the uninhabited Isle of Staffa inspired composer Felix Mendelssohn to write his *Hebrides Overture*.

▼ **Wild goat**

COUNTY FACTS

ARGYLL AND BUTE
Area: 6,930 sq km
Population: 90,550
Administrative centre:
Lochgilphead
Other key places: Campbeltown,
Dunoon, Inverary, Oban,
Port Ellen

EAST AYRSHIRE
Area: 1,252 sq km
Population: 124,000
Administrative centre:
Kilmarnock

EAST DUNBARTONSHIRE
Area: 172 sq km
Population: 110,220
Administrative centre:
Kirkintilloch

EAST RENFREWSHIRE
Area: 173 sq km
Population: 86,780
Administrative centre: Glasgow

INVERCLYDE
Area: 162 sq km
Population: 89,990
Administrative centre:
Greenock
Other key places: Gourock

NORTH AYRSHIRE
Area: 884 sq km
Population: 139,000
Administrative centre: Irvine
Other key places: Ardrossan,
Brodick

NORTH LANARKSHIRE
Area: 474 sq km
Population: 326,700
Administrative centre:
Motherwell
Other key places: Coatbridge

RENFREWSHIRE
Area: 261 sq km
Population: 177,000
Administrative centre: Paisley

SOUTH AYRSHIRE
Area: 1,202 sq km
Population: 114,000
Administrative centre: Ayr
Other key places: Alloway,
Ballantrae, Girvan

SOUTH LANARKSHIRE
Area: 1,771 sq km
Population: 307,100
Administrative centre: Hamilton
Other key places: Blantyre,
Kirkfieldbank, Lanark

WEST DUMBARTONSHIRE
Area: 162 sq km
Population: 97,790
Administrative centre:
Dumbarton

CITY OF GLASGOW
Area: 175 sq km
Population: 623,850

Mull
Dunstaffnage Castle
Oban
Orchy
Sound of Lorne
Jura
KILMARTIN VALLEY
Inverary Castle
Inverary
Lochgilphead
Argyll Forest Park
Gare Loch
Loch Lomond
Dunoon
Greenock
Dumbarton
Kirkintilloch
Glasgow Airport
Glasgow Cathedral
Glasgow
Motherwell
Paisley
Hamilton
Clyde
Lanark
Sound of Jura
Bute
KINTYRE
Ardrossan
Irvine
Firth of Clyde
Arran
Kilmarnock
Campbeltown
Ayr
LOWTHER HILLS
Mull of Kintyre
Girvan
Stinchar
Doon
NORTH CHANNEL
Ballantrae

▼ **Jet-skier**

LOCH LOMOND
This is the largest inland waterway in
Britain. There are 37 islands located in the
loch. Today, it is a popular destination
for holidaymakers. Long ago, the islands
provided hideouts for Christian monks.

G

F

E

D

C

B

A

7   6   5   4   3   2   1

▲ **Burns Monument**
This monument stands in Alloway, Ayrshire, which was the birthplace of Robert Burns. Scots celebrate the poet's birthday each January 25th (Burns Night), with feasting and poetry readings.

THERE WAS A PREHISTORIC SETTLEMENT on the site of modern Glasgow, but the city began to develop only after St Kentigern (also called St Mungo) founded a chapel there in AD543. He died at Glasgow. Argyll had been colonized by Celtish people (known as Scots) from Ireland (known as Scotia). The Scottish king, Kenneth MacAlpin, who ruled from 843 until 860, also reigned over the Picts of northern Scotland. The southern part of the region formed the kingdom of Strathclyde, whose people were ancient Britons. Their king, Malcolm II, ruled from 997 until 1005 and was the first king of all Scotland.

◀ **St Mungo's Museum**
Opened in 1993, St Mungo's Museum, Glasgow, has a collection of art related to world religions. There is a stunning Zen garden in the museum grounds.

▼ **Scottish heroine**
Flora MacDonald helped Bonnie Prince Charlie to escape Scotland after the Jacobite Rebellion in the 1700s. She disguised the Stuart prince as a maid for the journey. MacDonald's punishment was imprisonment in Dunstaffnage Castle on the shores of Loch Etive.

BRUCE AND THE SPIDER

Robert the Bruce freed Scotland from English rule and became king in 1306. At one stage in the war he was heavily defeated, and fled for safety to a cave on the Isle of Arran. He was in despair until he saw a spider try – and fail – to climb up its silk thread. The spider succeeded only on its seventh attempt. This inspired Bruce, and he went back to continue the fight. People thought this was just a legend until an arachnologist (a spider expert) examined the cave and found a species of spider that is famous for being a bad climber.

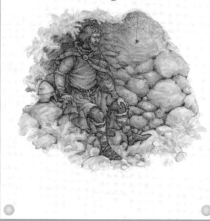

Castles

There has been a castle at Dumbarton since the 6th century, sited on a huge rock overlooking the river Clyde. Work on the castle at Rothesay, on the Isle of Bute, first began in the 1100s. The Vikings besieged the castle twice. The present building was largely rebuilt in the 1800s. Bothwell Castle was fought over by English and Scots, part of it being demolished in 1337.

◀ **Paisley patterns**
The town of Paisley, now in the suburbs of Glasgow, is famed for its patterned fabric. The swirling designs were copied from Indian Mughal art. Paisley became very popular in the 1960s.

▲ David Livingstone
This famous explorer and missionary was born in Blantyre, Lanarkshire. The first Westerner to visit central Africa, he named Victoria Falls after his queen.

▼ Campbell's castle
Archibald Campbell became Duke of Argyll in 1743. He rebuilt the family seat, Inverary Castle, and filled it with collections of books, porcelain and weaponry.

TOIL AND TROUBLE
One of Shakespeare's most famous tragedies is *Macbeth*. The 'Scottish play' tells how Macbeth, one of King Duncan's generals, kills Duncan to become king himself. Three witches that Macbeth met had foretold that he would be king. The real Macbeth died in 1057 and is said to lie buried on Iona.

Famous buildings
Inverary Castle, the seat of the dukes of Argyll, is a large house that was built in the late 1700s. It was designed to look like a French château. Culzean Castle in Ayrshire, another big house, was designed by Robert Adam. Hill House at Helensburgh was designed by Charles Rennie Mackintosh in 1902. Glasgow Cathedral, which dates from 1200, contains the remains of St Kentigern, and is dedicated to him under his nickname of St Mungo.

CAN YOU FIND?
1 Dunstaffnage Castle
2 Glasgow Cathedral
3 Iona
4 Loch Lomond
5 Paisley
6 Staffa

see page 19

▼ Glasgow School of Art
This building was designed inside and out by the architect Charles Rennie Mackintosh in the 1890s. Mackintosh's functional, geometric style is known as Art Nouveau.

Industry
Glasgow and the towns near it along the river Clyde make up Scotland's industrial heartland. The industries located there include shipbuilding, aircraft construction, iron and steel manufacture, and a wide variety of light engineering, especially in the 'new towns' of Cumbernauld, East Kilbride and Irvine. There are whisky distilleries in the region, for example on the Hebridean islands of Islay and Jura.

▲ Ayrshire dairy cattle

Farming
Agriculture plays a small part in the economy of Strathclyde. Farmers raise cattle and sheep, and there is a flourishing line of market gardening.

Central Scotland

T HE CENTRAL REGION OF SCOTLAND is made up the geographical counties of Stirlingshire, Clackmannanshire and part of Perthshire. Several important battles between the Scots and the English took place in this region, including the Battle of Bannockburn in 1314.

▼ Lomond's shore
Scotland's largest lake, Loch Lomond, forms the boundary between the Central and Strathclyde regions.

The region lies between the Highlands and the Lowlands. In the north are seven mountains reaching to heights of 900 metres or more. The highest area in the south is the Campsie Fells, made up of extinct, eroded volcanoes. To the east of Loch Lomond, along the southern fringes of the Highlands, lies the scenic Queen Elizabeth Forest, which includes the peak of Ben Lomond and six picturesque lochs.

▲ Fruity folly
When this carved stone folly was built at Dunmore Park, Stirlingshire, in 1761, the pineapple was a rare luxury. Today, the building is let to holidaymakers.

Towns and buildings

The region's main settlement is Stirling, crisscrossed by the river Forth. Overlooking the river and the city centre, on a nearby hill, is the tower built as a national monument to the medieval Scottish hero Sir William Wallace. On another hill stands Stirling Castle, which was captured by Wallace in 1297. The castle has been altered many times since it was built in the 13th century. In the north of the region is Finlarig Castle, built by the Campbell clan.

▼ The Battle of Bannockburn
In 1314 Robert the Bruce led a famous victory against the English at Bannockburn. This won Scotland's independence from England.

▲ The Trossachs
Tourists are attracted to the rugged scenery of Central Scotland. The glen between Lochs Achray and Katrine is known as the Trossachs.

Industry and farming

Most of the region's industry is based in the south. Grangemouth, on the Firth of Forth near Falkirk, has a large oil refinery. Nearby factories produce a wide range of manufactured goods. Whisky distilling and brewing are also important in the area. Farmers in the north of the region rear sheep; in the south, where the soil is better, crops are grown.

Moments in history

Stone Age people once lived on the banks of the river Forth. In AD141 the Romans built a wall across the region to mark the northern border of the mighty Roman Empire. It was called the Antonine Wall, after Emperor Antoninus Pius who ordered its construction. You can see remains of the wall near Falkirk.

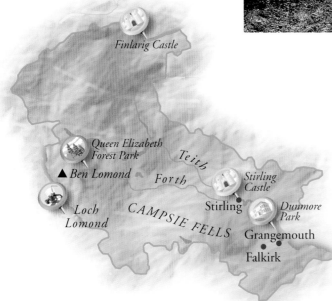

▲ Remains of the Antonine Wall

▲ Scottish thistle

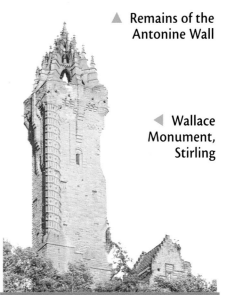

◄ Wallace Monument, Stirling

◄ **Castle Campbell**
This castle near Dollar, Clackmannanshire, dates to the 1400s. It was nicknamed 'Castle Gloom.'

WILLIAM WALLACE

Sir William Wallace is one of Scotland's great heroes. In the late 1200s he led the fight for Scottish independence from England. In 1297 he scored a victory at Stirling Bridge, but he was defeated at Falkirk the following year and escaped to France. On his return to Scotland he was betrayed to the English, and was hung, drawn and quartered, without trial, for the crime of treason. A monument to Wallace was built at Stirling in the 1800s.

Tayside and Fife

▼ River Tay

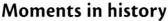

T HE MIGHTY RIVER TAY, the longest river in Scotland, dominates the region of Tayside and Fife. It flows through an area of rich, fertile farmland. The region includes the historic town of St Andrews, home to Scotland's oldest university and the most famous golf course in the world.

▲ Time for tee
The rules of golf were first drawn up in the clubhouse at St Andrews in 1754.

The river Tay, which flows across the region and out into the sea in the Firth of Tay, contains more water than any other river in the British Isles. The north and west of Tayside are mountainous, with the Grampian Mountains over in the northwest. There are several large lakes in the region, including Lochs Rannoch, Tummel, Tay and Leven. The land is flat and fertile in the south. Fife stretches out into the North Sea as a peninsula between the Firths of Tay and Forth.

▼ Scone
In AD838, Kenneth MacAlpin brought the Stone of Destiny to Scone, near Perth. Scottish kings were crowned on the Stone until the English carried it off in 1297.

Towns and industry

Dundee is the largest city in the region. It is an important engineering centre. Dundee is also famous for its marmalade and jam, but journalism is the biggest employer. Farther west, the city of Perth was once the capital of Scotland. This is an important farming area, and cattle rearing was widespread before the mad cow disease panic of the 1990s. Soft fruits are grown in the area, which is known for its raspberries and tayberries. There is fishing on the south coast, with the port of Arbroath famed for its 'smokies' (smoked haddock).

▲ Culross
In the 1600s, the village of Culross was an important trade centre for salt and coal. Today, it is a perfectly-preserved Scottish burgh with beautiful, painted cottages.

Moments in history

In the Middle Ages, Scotland's parliament met at Perth, which was the home of Scottish kings. During the English Civil War this area was involved in some heavy fighting. Fife became known as a kingdom because it was a separate, Pictish province. As recently as 1975, local people argued hard to keep Fife's own identity.

▶ Killicrankie Pass
This stunning gorge is just north of Pitlochry. At the spot called 'Soldiers' Leap,' Bonnie Dundee's Highland soldiers jumped across the Pass in 1689.

Castles

There are notable castles at Ravenscraig, St Andrews and Claypotts, where the castle is Z-shaped. Mary, Queen of Scots escaped from imprisonment in Loch Leven Castle. Princess Margaret was born at Glamis Castle, Angus, which was the childhood home of Queen Elizabeth, the Queen Mother. Long before her time, the Scottish king Macbeth lived at Glamis in the 11th century.

▼ **Tayberries**

▶ **Paint-a-Pict**
Some of the first people to live in this region were the Picts. Their name means 'painted people.' The Picts were renowned for their painted or tattooed bodies.

GRAMPIAN MOUNTAINS
Loch Rannoch
Loch Tummel
Tay Forest Park
● Pitlochry
Blairgowrie
● Montrose
● Forfar
Arbroath
Loch Tay
Tay
Claypotts Castle
St Andrews Cathedral
Dundee
Scone Palace
Scone
● Perth
● Crieff
Earn
Firth of Tay
St Andrews Bay
St Andrews Castle
St Andrews
OCHIL HILLS
Loch Leven
Glenrothes
Ravenscraig Castle
Kirkcaldy ●
Dunfermline
Firth of Forth

NORTH SEA

▼ **Dennis the Menace**

▶ **Gnasher**

SCHOOL
LIMEKILNS

◀ **In the smokehouse**
Haddock brought in to the port of Arbroath are cured to make the town's famous 'smokies.'

Grampian

▼ **Bred for beef**

The long coat of the Aberdeen Angus protects it from the harsh Scottish winters. The animal produces top-quality beef and is now raised around the world.

▼ **Speedy Spey**

Well-known for its salmon fishing, the Spey is also the fastest-flowing river in the British Isles.

THE GRAMPIAN REGION OCCUPIES the northeast corner of Scotland. Grampian includes the old geographical counties of Aberdeenshire, Banffshire, Kincardineshire and most of Morayshire. On the east coast of this mountainous region lies the port of Aberdeen, Scotland's third-largest city and centre of the Scottish oil industry.

The landscape of Grampian is dominated by the rugged Grampian Mountains. Several major rivers cut through this range, including tributaries of the river Spey which, at 172 kilometres long, is second only to the Tay in length and volume of water. Other rivers include the Deveron, Ythan, Don and Dee. The climate of this large region tends to be cool and windy, and snow lies on the mountains for much of the winter. The mountains shelter the rest of the region from the prevailing westerly rain-bearing winds.

▲ **Granite city**

Robert the Bruce rewarded Aberdeen's loyalty with a Common Good Fund. To this day, money from the fund is spent on beautifying the grey-granite city with dazzling flower displays.

Industry

Industry is mostly in the university city of Aberdeen, which lies at the mouth of the river Dee. The city was a bustling port as long ago as Viking times; today, it still has trade links with Scandinavia and the Baltic. Most importantly, though, it is a base for supplying and servicing oil platforms and drilling rigs in the North Sea. Aberdeen, Peterhead (another North-Sea oil centre), Buckie and Fraserburgh are key centres of Scotland's fishing industry. Whisky is distilled in the region, too: the town of Dufftown has seven working distilleries, including the famous Glenfiddich Distillery.

▼ **Tug-o'-war**

Near to the Queen's holiday residence, Balmoral, is the village of Braemar. The Highland Games are held at Braemar every August.

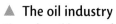

▲ **The oil industry**

Since the oil boom of the 1970s and 1980s, offshore oil rigs have drilled the North Sea for precious supplies of oil.

Farming

Grampian is Scotland's leading farming region, producing barley, oats and wheat. Aberdeen Angus cattle are bred here. There are around 1,000 square kilometres of managed forests.

Moments in history

There are remains of Stone Age and Iron Age peoples across Grampian, including stone circles and hill forts. The region was part of the Pictish kingdom at various times. Celtic missionaries founded monasteries in the area in the 1st millennium AD. Among them was St Machar, an Irish-born bishop who founded the first church in what later became Aberdeen. The present-day twin-towered cathedral of St Machar stands on the site.

NORTH SEA

Buckie · Banff · Fraserburgh · *Kinnairds Head*

Elgin · Keith · Turriff · Peterhead

Spey · *Deveron* · *Ythan*

Inverurie · *Aberdeen Airport* · *Aberdeen Cathedral*

Don · *Craigievar Castle* · Aberdeen

CAIRNGORM MOUNTAINS · *Balmoral Castle* · Ballater · *Dee*

Braemar · GRAMPIAN MOUNTAINS · *Dunnottar Castle* · Stonehaven

COUNTY FACTS

ABERDEENSHIRE
Area: 6,311 sq km
Population: 223,630
Administrative centre: Aberdeen
Other key places: Braemar, Fraserburgh, Stonehaven

MORAY
Area: 2,238 sq km
Population: 86,250
Administrative centre: Elgin
Other key places: Buckie, Keith

CITY OF ABERDEEN
Area: 186 sq km
Population: 218,220

CASTLES

BALMORAL CASTLE, ABERDEENSHIRE
Rebuilt during the 1800s, this is a private house belonging to the Queen.

CRAIGIEVAR CASTLE, ABERDEENSHIRE
This tall, graceful castle has fairytale towers and turrets of pink granite.

DUNNOTTAR CASTLE, ABERDEENSHIRE
Dunnottar stands on the cliffs near Stonehaven. The Scottish crown and sceptre (known as the 'Honours of Scotland') were hidden here during the English Civil War.

HUNTLY CASTLE, ABERDEENSHIRE
This ruined castle was once home to the Gordon clan. Above the doorway is a carving showing Christ, St Michael and the royal coat of arms.

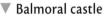

▼ Balmoral castle

▲ **Barrels of whisky**
The Glenfiddich Distillery produces millions of bottles of single-malt whisky each year. The spirit, made from fermented barley, is aged in oak casks. These are handmade by Glenfiddich's own coopers (barrel-makers).

G
F
E
D
C
B
A

Highland

This monument marks the events of February 13, 1692. Soldiers from the Campbell clan were staying with the MacDonalds at Glencoe. They slaughtered 38 of their hosts, on the orders of William III.

▼ Ben Nevis
At 1,343 metres, this is the highest peak in the whole British Isles.

THE HIGHLAND REGION reaches to the northernmost tip of the Scottish mainland at John o'Groats. Although Highland covers a vast area, there are only eight people per square kilometre. It is a region of great beauty, with deep glens, rugged mountains and wild moors.

Most of Highland consists of the Northwest Highlands, plus some lowland areas along the north and east coasts and the Isle of Skye to the west. The mainland part of the region is split by Glen Mor (the Great Glen), a huge fault valley which runs from southwest to northeast. The valley contains a chain of lakes, from the sea loch of Loch Linnhe in the south, continuing with Lochs Lochy, Oich and Ness, and ending at the Moray Firth. The artificial Caledonian Canal links these lochs. Dozens of other lochs are strewn across the region, many opening directly to the sea.

▼ Caithness glass
The glass-blowing factory at Thurso makes beautiful paper-weights and vases.

Industry and farming

The region has no major cities: the largest place is the market town of Inverness. The most important industry is manufacturing equipment for the North Sea oil fields. There are aluminium smelters near Fort William and Kinlochleven, and textile mills and whisky distilleries. Apart from sheep-rearing on the hills, there is only limited farming. Large herds of wild deer are culled to provide venison, while fish farms produce salmon.

▼ Monster of the deep
Loch Ness is home of a legendary monster, Nessie. Eyewitnesses describe a creature that looks like a prehistoric plesiosaur.

Moments in history

Around the AD500s the west coast of this region was colonized by Scots from Ireland. Later, Vikings settled in the coastal areas. From about AD1000 Highlanders were organized into clans – families with the same surnames. Sometimes, clan warfare broke out. The last battle on British soil took place in Highland in 1746 – the Battle of Culloden.

◄ Plesiosaur

Portree ●

Skye

CUILLI
HILLS

Canna

Rhum

Eigg

▶ Dunvesan Castle
Home to the chief clan of Skye, the MacLeods, Dunvesan Castle dates to the 9th century.

9

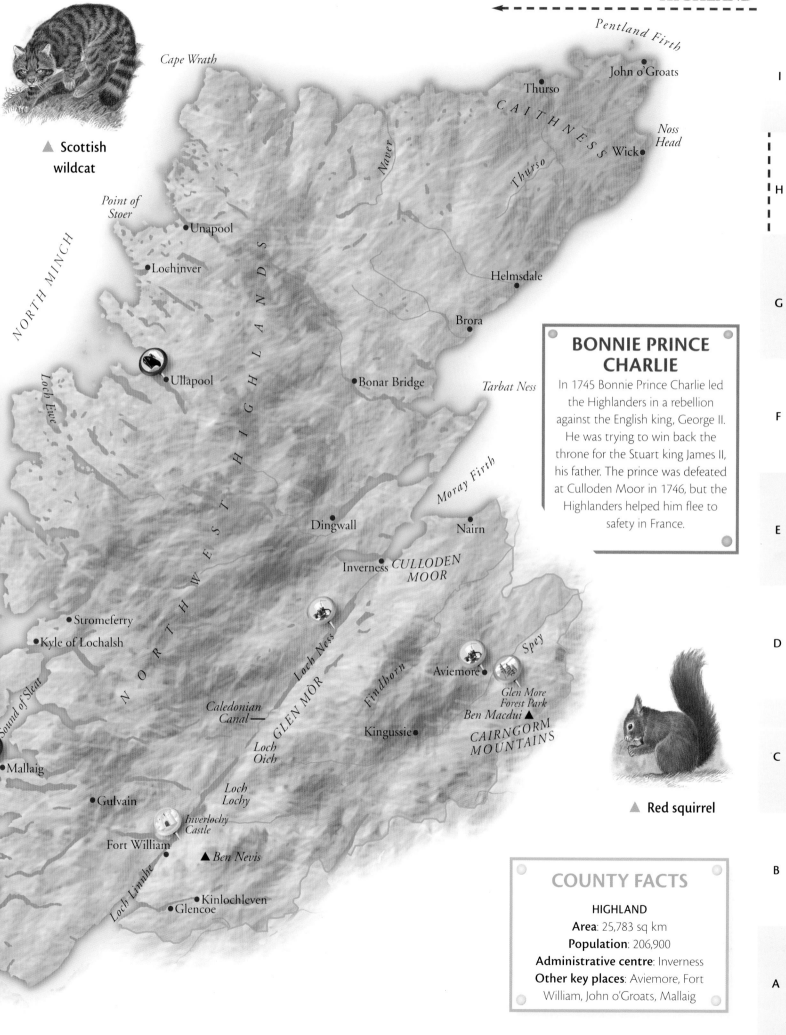

Pentland Firth

I

Cape Wrath

John o'Groats

Thurso

C A I T H N E S S

Naver

Thurso

H

▲ Scottish
wildcat

*Point of
Stoer*

Unapool

Wick

*Noss
Head*

NORTH MINCH

Lochinver

Helmsdale

G

Loch Ewe

Brora

Ullapool

Bonar Bridge

Tarbat Ness

BONNIE PRINCE CHARLIE

In 1745 Bonnie Prince Charlie led the Highlanders in a rebellion against the English king, George II. He was trying to win back the throne for the Stuart king James II, his father. The prince was defeated at Culloden Moor in 1746, but the Highlanders helped him flee to safety in France.

F

Moray Firth

Dingwall

Nairn

E

Stromeferry

Inverness

*CULLODEN
MOOR*

NORTH WEST HIGHLANDS

Loch Ness

Spey

D

Kyle of Lochalsh

GLEN MOR

Findhorn

Aviemore

*Glen More
Forest Park*

Ben Macdui ▲

Sound of Sleat

*Caledonian
Canal*

Kingussie

*CAIRNGORM
MOUNTAINS*

*Loch
Oich*

▲ Red squirrel

Mallaig

*Loch
Lochy*

Gulvain

*Inverlochy
Castle*

Fort William

▲ Ben Nevis

B

Loch Linnhe

Kinlochleven

Glencoe

COUNTY FACTS

HIGHLAND
Area: 25,783 sq km
Population: 206,900
Administrative centre: Inverness
Other key places: Aviemore, Fort William, John o'Groats, Mallaig

A

The Western Isles

THE WESTERN ISLES are a group of islands off the northwest coast of Scotland. They are also known as the Outer Hebrides. Many of the islands are very small and are uninhabited. The largest island is Lewis with Harris (Lewis is the northern part). Regular ferries link the islanders with mainland Scotland. Many inhabitants of the Western Isles still speak Scottish Gaelic as their first language.

To the south of Lewis with Harris are the three islands of North Uist, Benbecula and South Uist, which are linked by bridges. Farther south are Eriskay and Barra, which are reached by a ferry service. There are several smaller islands, including the uninhabited St Kilda group, 64 kilometres to the west. The Western Isles are mostly mountainous, with large areas of open moorland and rolling, grassy plains. Sea lochs indent the craggy coastline, and there are hundreds of small, freshwater lochs inland. A range of hills divides Lewis from Harris, which ends in a long peninsula. The two are connected by a strip of land with a sea loch on either side.

Industry and farming

The chief industry of the islands is the production of Harris tweed. Some is manufactured in mills at Stornoway, the chief town, but most is made in the homes of local crofters. There are 5,500 crofts (smallholdings) on the islands, where sheep and cattle are raised and potatoes are grown. Yet less than six percent of the land is suitable for farming. Fishing fleets catch shellfish and a few herrings and whitefish. Tourism and fish farming, mainly of salmon, are growing industries.

▼ Celtic cross
There are 54 prehistoric standing stones at Callanish, Lewis. The stones are arranged in the shape of a cross.

▼ Whalebones
At Bragar, on Lewis, two whalebones form an arch by the side of the road. Hanging from the top of the arch is the harpoon used to kill the whale.

▲ Black house
At Eochar, South Uist, you can still find some thatched 'black houses.' Crofters lived in these Viking-style longhouses until the 1930s. Each turf-built house had a central, peat-burning fire but no chimney.

▲ Fishing boats
At low tide, the islanders' fishing boats are beached on the Island of Lewis.

◄ Bleak and black
The landscape of Lewis is dominated by the Black Moor. This peaty moorland is scattered with many tiny lochs.

Moments in history

There are several stone circles in the Western Isles, including Callanish which was begun 4,000 years ago. It is the largest prehistoric monument on the islands and has a central burial chamber. In the 9th century Vikings settled the islands, which were claimed by Norway until 1266. Three clans ruled the islands until after the Jacobite rising of 1745, when they came under the control of the United Kingdom government. Overpopulation and poverty caused many islanders to emigrate to America and Australia in the 1800s.

▼ **Seilebost, Island of Harris**
Tourists are attracted to the islands' stunning white-sand beaches, which rival any in the Caribbean. Unfortunately, the weather does not!

Butt of Lewis

H

Callanish
Stornoway

Eye Peninsula

G

Lewis

ATLANTIC OCEAN

E

St KILDA

Harris

North Minch

COUNTY FACTS

**COUNCIL OF THE WESTERN ISLES
(COMHAIRLE NAN EILEAN SIAR)**
Area: 3,134 sq km
Population: 29,410
Administrative centre: Stornoway
Other key places: Callanish

North Uist

D

Benbecula

Little Minch

South Uist

C

▼ **Harris tweed**

Kisimul Castle   *Barra*

SEA OF THE HEBRIDES

B

GIFT TO A GOD

During the 1600s, islanders on Lewis made sure to perform this special rite on October 31st each year. Someone would wade into the sea, chanting to call up the sea god, Shony. They offered the god a cup of ale in the hope of a good crop of seaweed. They used seaweed to fertilize their fields.

A

Orkney

▼ **Prepare to dive**
Scapa Flow is Europe's best diving site. Wrecks in the clear waters include three German battleships, sunk during World War I, and HMS *Royal Oak*, sunk during World War II.

THE ORKNEY ISLANDS LIE TEN KILOMETRES from the northeastern tip of mainland Scotland. The Orkney chain contains about 90 islands – as well as numerous holms (islets) and skerries (rocky reefs) – but only 21 of the islands are inhabited. Together with the Shetland Islands, the Orkneys make up the boundary between the North Sea and the Atlantic Ocean.

▲ **Bird-watchers' paradise**
Steep cliffs on the tiny island of Copinsay provide nesting nooks for many types of seabird, including guillemots (*above*) and kittiwakes.

The Orkneys are separated from Scotland's north coast by a narrow channel called the Pentland Firth. There are steep cliffs on the west and south coasts of the islands, while the north and east coasts are jagged. Inland, the landscape is mostly low-lying, with rocks, swamps and small lochs. Much of the ground is peat-based, but there is some rich arable land. The climate is mild, with plenty of rainfall.

◀ **Old Man of Hoy**
This spectacular rock stack towers up to a height of 137 metres.

Important places

The largest island, Mainland, has two towns: Kirkwall, the capital, and the port of Stromness. The second-largest island is Hoy, which is part of a group called the South Isles. Off its rugged cliffs stands a detached rocky pillar known as the Old Man of Hoy. To the south, the islands of Burray and South Ronaldsay are linked to Mainland by causeways known as the Churchill Barriers. They were built during World War II to protect the waters of Scapa Flow, which were used by the Royal Navy.

▼ **Prehistoric grave**
Built around 2750BC, Maes Howe was designed so the Sun's rays shone into the central chamber at the winter solstice. Vikings plundered the site and you can still see their runic graffiti on the chamber walls!

▼ **Ring of Brodgar**
This 91-metre-wide circle of standing stones was erected on Mainland during the Bronze Age. Thirty-six of the original 60 stones reach skywards to this day.

Industry and farming

Fishing, farming and craft industries are the main occupations of the Orkneys. The chief agricultural products are beef, dairy products, eggs and barley. Barley is malted at the Highland Park Distillery, Kirkwall, to make single-malt whisky. There is a North-Sea oil terminal on the island of Flotta. Air and sea services link the islands, and connect them with Shetland and the mainland of Scotland.

▲ **School air-bus**
Kirkwall airport operates a daily link to the Scottish mainland. Orcadian children have to take the plane to and from school!

Moments in history

Stone Age and Bronze Age peoples lived in Orkney, and they have left behind stone circles, underground houses and standing stones. The Romans knew the islands as the Orcades. Denmark owned the Orkney Islands from the AD800s until 1472. In that year the Scottish king, James III, married a Danish princess and the islands, along with the Shetlands, formed part of her marriage dowry.

Westray
North Ronaldsay
Rousay
Sanday
Mainland
Stronsay
Skara Brae ■
Kirkwall Cathedral
Shapinsay
Stromness •
• Kirkwall
NORTH SEA
Hoy
Scapa Flow
South Ronaldsay
Pentland Firth

COUNTY FACTS

ORKNEY
Area: 992 sq km
Population: 19,760
Administrative centre: Kirkwall
Other key places: Stromness

SKARA BRAE

Skara Brae is a 5,000-year-old village on Mainland. It was preserved under sand from 2500BC, until a storm revealed it again in 1851. The walls of the huts – and the furniture, too – were built of stone slabs, because the Orkneys have few trees. By examining the remains, experts now know that the villagers grew barley and wheat, and raised cattle and sheep. They also caught seafood and hunted wild game.

▲ **Leatherback turtles**

Shetland

▼ Shetland pony
The world's smallest breed of horse, the Shetland pony, stands just over a metre tall.

▼ Muckle Flugga lighthouse, Unst
David Stevenson built Britain's most northerly lighthouse in 1854. His nephew, author Robert Louis Stevenson, stayed here to write his famous novel *Treasure Island*.

THE SHETLAND ISLANDS (also known as Zetland) are the most northerly part of the British Isles. They lie 80 kilometres northeast of Orkney, and nearly 200 kilometres off the Scottish mainland. The nearest mainland town is Bergen, in Norway.

There are about 100 islands and islets, but less than 20 of them are inhabited. The largest island is Mainland, where more than half the people live. The other large islands are Yell, Unst, Feltar, Whalsay and Bressay. Fair Isle lies 40 kilometres south of the main group. Only about 100 people live there. Shetland is bleak, consisting mostly of moorland with few trees. The coasts are rocky, and are broken up by long sea lochs called 'voes.' The highest point is Ronas Hill (450 metres) on Mainland. The climate is humid and fairly mild, but the weather is always windy and there are often gales.

▼ Sullom Voe
This massive oil terminal is Europe's biggest. Two 160-km-long underwater pipelines carry crude oil there from the North-Sea oilfields.

Industry

North Sea oil has brought much-needed work to the Shetlanders. There is a huge oil terminal at Sullom Voe. Sumburgh Airport, on the southern tip of Mainland, operates a helicopter service out to the oil rigs, as well as services to the mainland cities of Aberdeen and Inverness.

▼ Ness Yole
This boat used for inshore fishing shows the influence of the Vikings, or Norsemen. Shetland was part of Norway from the 800s to the 1400s.

Farming

Agriculture in Shetland is limited because of poor soil and rugged land. Most farmers work on crofts (smallholdings) and rear sheep. Shetland sheep produce fine-quality wool which is hand-knitted by the islanders. Hardy Shetland ponies are reared on Unst and some of the other islands. Fishing boats bring in catches of herring and whitefish to the ports of Lerwick and Scalloway. Fish farming is a growing industry.

▲ Fair Isle tank top
An authentic Fair Isle knit must have been made on Fair Isle itself and have the distinctive OXOXO patterning.

Herma Ness

Unst

Yell

Fetlar

Scatsta Airport ●Sullom Voe

St Magnus Bay

Whalsay

Papa Stour

Mainland

NORTH SEA

Lerwick Castle
●Lerwick

Foula

Fair Isle

Moments in history

The earliest inhabitants of the Shetland Islands were prehistoric, and they have left behind many remains, including stone circles. The site of Jarlshof, in the south of Mainland, shows signs of continuous settlement over several centuries. There is a group of Bronze Age houses which were built in the 700s BC. Viking settlers arrived in the 8th century AD, and most Shetlanders today are of Norse descent. The islands belonged to Norway until 1472, when they were annexed to Scotland along with the Orkneys.

▲ **Jarlshof**
This prehistoric and Viking settlement was uncovered by a gale in the early 1900s.

▼**Up-Helly-Aa**

Glossary

Act of Union A law passed in parliament to join two (or more) countries together.

Anglo Saxon Relating to the Germanic peoples (including Angles, Saxons and Jutes) who settled England and Scotland.

arable Describes land used for growing crops rather than, for example, raising cows or sheep.

basalt A type of very hard, dark-coloured igneous rock.

Bronze Age The prehistoric time after the Stone Age, lasting from around 2300BC until 700BC, when people used bronze for tools and weapons.

devolution A type of home rule, where some parts of government are controlled locally instead of by the national parliament.

canal A man-made river, usually almost perfectly flat, that can be used to transport goods by boat.

causeway A raised road or pathway, for example over marshy land, or across a stretch of sea.

Celt A member of one of the prehistoric tribes of farmers that settled Britain and Ireland during the Iron Age. Celtic languages, such as Gaelic, are still alive today in Ireland, Wales, the Scottish Highlands and the Isle of Man.

clan Like a tribe, a group of people led by a single chieftain, especially in the Scottish Highlands. Clan members are often related and share the same surname.

climate The average weather of a place throughout the year.

continental drift The gradual movement of the Earth's land masses that breaks up existing continents and forms new ones.

crannog Gaelic word describing an artifical island on which a dwelling or fort has been built.

croft A smallholding, usually consisting of a tiny farm with a cottage.

cromlech A prehistoric stone structure, such as a tomb or standing stones.

dale Low-lying ground between hills; often, this is a river valley.

dam A large wall or bank built to hold back river water and raise its level.

distilling Process of purifying an alcoholic drink, such as whisky, by evaporating and condensing it.

dolmen A prehistoric stone structure, probably used as a tomb. It usually consisted of several standing stones with a flat stone placed on top.

earthwork A mound of earth used in prehistoric times as a fort.

erode To wear away the land. Wind, moving water and glaciers all erode the land.

escarpment The steep side of a hill, cliff or rock.

estuary The part of a river where it reaches the sea and often has tides; the river's mouth.

fault A crack in the rocks that form the Earth's crust. Fault lines are likely spots for earthquakes or volcanoes.

fell A hill, usually of uncultivated land such as pasture or moor.

firth The mouth of a river or an arm of the sea.

fishery A place where fish are caught.

flax Fibres from the *Linum* plant, used to make linen.

game Wild animals killed for food or sport, such as deer (for venison meat), geese or rabbits.

gasfield An area that has deposits of natural gas.

glacier A large sheet of ice, or ice and rock, that flows slowly down a valley like a frozen river.

glen A narrow, often wooded, valley.

gorge A deep, narrow canyon that cuts through the land.

granite A type of very hard, speckled igneous rock.

grove A small area of woodland.

Gulf Stream Warm water current that originates in the Gulf of Mexico and flows across the Atlantic to northwestern Europe.

headland A point of land that juts out into the sea.

hill fort A prehistoric stronghold on top of a hill.

home rule Self-government, as opposed to rule by another country.

hummock A small hill.

hydroelectric power Energy made by harnessing the movement of water, either downhill or in tides or waves.

igneous Describes a rock formed when volcanic lava cooled. Granite and basalt are both igneous rocks.

Industrial Revolution Period when the first factories were built. Instead of human labour, newly-invented, steam-powered machines performed repetitive or heavy tasks. In Britain, this began in the 1760s.

Iron Age The prehistoric time after the Bronze Age, beginning around 700BC, when people used iron tools and weapons.

inlet A small bay in a coastline.

islet A tiny island.

kirk A Scottish word for 'church.'

limestone A type of easily-eroded rock, such as chalk, that formed millions of years ago from the crushed shells and skeletons of tiny sea creatures.

loch Pronounced 'lock'. A Gaelic word meaning 'lake.' A loch may contain fresh or salt water.

managed forest Trees planted rather like a crop to be harvested for their timber. Felled trees are replaced with new saplings.

marina A harbour or dock where yachts are berthed.

market garden A garden where fruit, vegetables and flowers are grown for sale to the public.

medieval From the Middle Ages.

Middle Ages The time between the end of the Roman empire in the AD400s, until the explosion of invention and learning in the 1400s, known as the Renaissance.

mint A place where money is printed or coined.

monarch A head of state, for example a king or queen, who inherits their title.

moorland An expanse of wild, uncultivated land, which often has poor, peaty soil.

motte-and-bailey castle A type of castle built by the Normans, where the tower, or keep, is built on an earth mound (motte), surrounded by a walled courtyard (bailey).

national assembly An assembly of elected representatives that governs a country, or aspects of a country.

oil platform A steel or concrete structure that supports an oil rig out at sea. Some platforms are free-floating; others are fixed to the seabed.

oil rig The machinery and structures used to drill for oil.

outcrop Rock that is visible at the surface, rather than hidden under the soil.

paramilitary Describes a rebel group that is organized like an army.

parliament The seat of government. Some members of parliament are elected by the people (in Britain, they attend the House of Commons; in the Republic of Ireland, they attend the Dáil); others are born or appointed to a position in the upper house (in Britain, this is the House of Lords; in the Republic of Ireland, this is the Senate).

patron saint A saint considered to be protector of a country.

peat bog Marshy land where peat has formed. Peat is long-decayed vegetation, the first step in the process that produces coal.

pele tower A simple, fortified house, often entered by means of a ladder to the first floor.

Pict A prehistoric Celtic people that inhabited northeastern Scotland.

plain An area of flat or gently-undulating land, usually low-lying.

plantation of Ireland The settling of Ireland from the 1600s by English and Scottish people, so Britain could establish control.

plateau An area of level, high ground.

plug Rock that has hardened inside a volcano's central hole, or vent.

pothole A deep hole eroded in limestone.

prehistoric From the time before there were any written historical records.

prevailing wind The wind that blows most often in a particular place or region.

principality A territory ruled by a prince or princes.

Protestant Church A branch of Christianity that has separated from the Roman Catholic Church. Protestant churches first formed during the Reformation.

province A distinct part of a country, treated differently to the rest of the country.

reef A chain of underwater rocks, usually closer to the surface than the surrounding seabed.

refinery A place where raw ingredients are processed, for example an oil or sugar refinery.

regeneration The creation of new buildings and businesses in a place.

republic A country without a monarch as head of state, that is governed entirely by elected representatives of the people.

Roman Catholic Church The first Christian Church, headed by the Pope in Rome. Catholic means 'universal.'

rune A symbol that is a character, or letter, from one of the alphabets used by Germanic peoples between the 3rd and 13th centuries.

slate Shiny, green- or blue-grey rock made up of thin plates, often used for roofing tiles.

smallholding A small plot of land, usually used for farming.

smokehouse A place where meat, fish or cheese is smoked, usually over a wood fire.

solar power Energy from the Sun.

solstice The day that the Sun is farthest away from the Equator. This happens twice in a year on the longest and shortest days, June 21st and December 21st.

stack An isolated pillar of rock, usually poking out of the sea.

standing stone A huge stone set upright in the ground. They were erected by prehistoric peoples, probably for religious purposes.

Stone Age The prehistoric time before the Bronze Age, from around 4000BC until 2300BC, when people used tools and weapons made of stone, such as flint. The period is split into the Old Stone Age (Paleolithic) and New Stone Age (Neolithic).

stone circle A ring of prehistoric standing stones.

supertanker A huge boat that carries a liquid cargo, such as oil.

suspension bridge A bridge with its deck supported from above by large cables or chains hanging from towers.

tributary A stream or river that flows into – and becomes part of – another, larger river.

tweed Rough, woollen cloth. Much of it is produced in the valley of the river Tweed.

Viking A Scandinavian people who invaded or raided parts of Britain between the AD700s and 1000s.

volcano A vent in the Earth's crust, out of which molten rock, ashes and steam erupt.

wetland Marshy land.

wold A low hill.

MAP CO-ORDINATES

Co-ordinates provide a way to find a place on a map. On each map page there is a border at the bottom that is divided into numbered blocks, and a border at the edge that is divided into lettered blocks. Together with the page number, these border numbers and letters are used to create the co-ordinates.

How do I give a place on a map its own co-ordinates?

1 Write down the page that the place is on. This is the first co-ordinate. If you want co-ordinates for Glasgow, then '19' is the first part, because Glasgow appears on the map on page 19.

2 Next put your finger on the place itself. Trace down to the bottom of the page and see which numbered block you reach. This number is the second co-ordinate. In the case of Glasgow, you reach number '4.'

3 Now put your finger back on the place and trace across to the edge of the page to see which lettered block you reach. This is the last co-ordinate. In the case of Glasgow, you reach letter 'D.'

4 Write down the three co-ordinates, separating them with commas so that they don't get muddled together. The co-ordinates for Glasgow would be '19, 4, D.'

Index

Numbers in *italics* refer to illustrations.

A

Abbotsford 15
Aberdeen 26, *26*, 27
    Common Good Fund 26
Aberdeen Angus Cattle 9, 26, *26*
Aberdeenshire 27
Act of Union 6
Alloway 20
animal feed 12, 14
Angus 25
Antonine Wall 23, *23*
Arbroath 24, 25
Argyll 18
Argyll and Bute 19
Aviemore *8*

B

Balmoral Castle 27, *27*
Barra 30
Bass Rock 16
Battle of Bannockburn 7, *22*
Battle of Culloden 28, 29
Battle of Flodden 11
Beano 25
Ben Lomond 22
Ben Nevis *6*, 28
Benbecula 30
Berwick-upon-Tweed 15
bird colonies and reserves 17, *32*
Black Agnes 17, *17*
black houses *30*
Black Moor *30*
Blackhope Scar 16
Bonnie Prince Charlie 20, *29*
Borders 14–15
Bothwell Castle 20
Braemar 26
Bragar *30*
brewing 10, 22
Burns, Robert *13*, 20
Burns Night 20
Burnswark 13

C

Caerlaverock Castle *12*
Cairnholy 12
Caithness glass 28
Callanish *30*, 31
Campsie Fells 22
Castle Campbell *23*
Central Lowlands 8
Central Scotland 22–23
Cheviot Hills 8, 14

Church of Scotland 7
Churchill Barriers 32
City of Aberdeen 27
City of Dundee 25
City of Edinburgh 17
City of Glasgow 19
Clackmannanshire 23
clans 28
climate 9
Clyde river 18
Coldstream Guards *14*
comics 25
continental drift 8, *8*
Copinsay 32
Council of the Western Isles 31
Craigievar Castle 27
Culross *24*
Culzean Castle 21
currency 7

D

distilleries, whisky 10, 28, 32
    Glenfiddich 26, *27*
    Islay and Jura 21
doocots (dovecots) *16*
Dumbarton Castle 20
Dumfries and Galloway 12–13
Dunbar Castle 17
Dundee 24, 25
Dunmore Park *22*
Dunnottar Castle 27
Dunoon *18*
Duns Scotus 15, *15*
Dunstaffnage Castle 20
Dunvesan Castle 28

E

East Ayrshire 19
East Dunbartonshire 19
East Lothian 17
East Renfrewshire 19
Edinburgh 10–11, 17
    Arthur's Seat 10
    Bobby the Skye terrier *10*
    Castle 10, *11*
    Flodden Wall 11
    International Festival of Music and
    Dance *10*
    Military Tattoo *11*
    Museum of Scotland 10
    National Monument *10*
    Palace of Holyroodhouse 10, *10*
    places of interest 11
    Royal Mile *11*
    St Giles' Cathedral 7
    University *11*
    Water of Leith *11*
    electronics 16

Emperor Antoninus Pius 23
Eochar *30*
Eriskay 90
Ettrick Forest 14
Eyemouth *14*

F

Fair Isle 34
    knits *34*
Falkirk 23
farming
    pigs 12
    cattle 12, 14, 21, 33
    arable and crops 12, 17, 22, 26
    sheep 12, 14, 17, 21, 22, 34
festival of fire 35
Fife 25
Fingal's Cave *18*
Firth of Forth 9, 10, *16*
fish farming 30, 34
fishing 12, 24, 30, 34
Flotta 33
football teams 21
forests 26
Forth Rail Bridge 16, *17*
Forth river 9, 10, 22
Forth Road Suspension Bridge 16, 17
fruit, soft 24

G

George II 29
Glamis Castle 25
Glasgow 18, 19, 20
    Cathedral 21
    George Square *18*
    Glasgow School of Art *21*
    St Mungo's Museum 20
glass 28
Glen Mor 9, 18, 28
Glencoe 28
golf 24, *24*
government 7
Grampian 26–27
Grampian Mountains 24, 26
Great Glen 9, 18, 28
Greenknowe Tower 15
Gretna Green 12

H

Harris 30, *31*
heavy industry 21
Hebrides Overture 18
Highland 28–29
Highland Games 26
Highlanders 28, 29
Highlands 8
history 6
Holyroodhouse, Palace of 10, *10*

Huntly Castle 27
hydroelectric power stations 12, *12*

I

Inverary Castle 21
Inverclyde 19
Isle of Mull *18*
Isle of Skye 28

J

James III 6
James IV 11
James VI 6
    family tree 7
Jarlshof 35, *35*
John o'Groats 28
journalism 24

K

Killicrankie Pass *24*
Kirkwall 32, 33
knits, Fair Isle *34*
Knox, John *7*

L

language 7, 30
Lewis with Harris 30, *30*, 31
    rite 31
lighthouse 34
Linlithgow Palace *17*
Livingston 16
Livingstone, David *21*
Loch Duich *8*
Loch Leven Castle 25
Loch Lomond 18, 19, *22*
Loch Ness 28
lochs 8, 18, 28
Lothian 6–7

M

MacAlpin, Kenneth 6, 20, 24
Macbeth 21, 25
Macbeth 21
MacDonald, Flora *20*
Mackintosh, Charles Rennie *21*
Maes Howe *32*
Mainland (Orkney) 32
Mainland (Shetland) 34
Malcolm II 6
marine mammals *18*
market gardening 17, 21
Mary, Queen of Scots 17, 25
Meickle, Andrew *16*
Melrose Abbey *14*
Mendelssohn, Felix 18
Merse 14
Midlothian 17
monks 12, 19

Moray 27
mountains 8, *8*, 9, 22
Muckle Flugga lighthouse *34*
Mull of Galloway 12

N
national emblem 6
ness yole *34*
Nessie *28*
North Ayrshire 19
North Lanarkshire 19
North Uist 30

O
oil 22, *26*, 28, 33, 34
Old Man of Hoy 32, *32*
Orcades 33
Orkney 32–33
Outer Hebrides 30

P
Paisley *20*
Parliament 7, 10
patron saint 6
Pentland Firth 32
Pentland Hills 16
Perth 24
Perth & Kinross 25
physical features 8–9
Picts *6*, 20, 25
power stations 12, *12*

R
rain shadow 9
reivers *15*
religions 7
Renfrewshire 19
Rhinns of Galloway 12
Ring of Brodgar *32*
Robert the Bruce 6, *7*, 12, *20*, 22
rocks 9
Rothesay Castle 20
royal emblem 6
runes *12*
Ruthwell Cross *12*

S
St Andrew *6*
St Andrews *24*
St Kentigern 20, 21
St Kilda group 30
St Machar 27
St Mungo 20, 21
St Ninian 13
salmon *12*
Scapa Flow *32*
Scone 24
Scots 20, *28*

Scott, Sir Walter 14, 15, *18*
Seilebost *31*
Shakespeare, William 21
Shetland 34–35
Shetland pony *34*
Skara Brae 33, *33*
skiing *8*
smokies 24, *25*
South Ayrshire 19
South Lanarkshire 19
South Uist 30
Southern Uplands 8, 14
Spey river 26, *26*
standing stones *30*, *32*
Stevenson, Robert Louis 34
Stewarts 6
Stirling 22
   Castle 22
Stirlingshire 23
stone circles 31
Stone of Destiny *24*
Stranraer 12
Strathclyde 18–21
Stromness 32
Sullom Voe 34, *34*
Sweetheart Abbey *12*

T
Tay river *6*, 24, *24*
Tayside and Fife 24–25
textiles 14, 28
thistle *6*
Thomson,DC 25
Threave Castle *13*
threshing machine *16*
Trossachs *22*
tweed 14
   Harris 30, *31*
Tweed river 14, *14*

U
universities 11, 18
Up-Helly-Aa 35, *35*

V
Vikings 13, *13*

W
Wallace, Sir William 22, 23, *23*
Waverley novels 15
West Dumbartonshire 19
West Lothian 17
Western Isles, The 30–31
whalebones *30*
whisky *see* distilleries

Z
Zetland 34

'CAN YOU FIND?' answers

Scotland: Strathclyde p21

1	Dunstaffnage Castle	19, 6, G
2	Glasgow Cathedral	19, 4, D
3	Iona	18, 8, F
4	Loch Lomond	19, 4, E
5	Paisley	19, 4, D
6	Staffa	18, 8, F

Acknowledgements

The publishers would like to thank the following artists whose work appears in this title:

Lisa Alderton/Advocate, Vanessa Card, Kuo Kang Chen; Wayne Ford, Terry Gabbey/AFA Ltd., Jeremy Gower, Ron Hayward, Gary Hincks, Sally Holmes, Richard Hook/Linden Artists, The Maltings, Janos Marffy, Terry Riley, Andrew Robinson, Peter Sarson, Mike Saunders, Christian Webb/Temple Rogers, Mike White/Temple Rogers, John Woodcock.

PHOTOGRAPHIC CREDITS

The publishers thank the following sources for the use of their photographs:

6 (B/L) Sant'Emidio, Ascoli Picena, Bridgeman Art Library; 7 (B/L) S.J.Taylor/Still Moving Picture Co.; 8 (T/R) Cairngorm Marketing; 10, (B/L) Doug Corrance/Still Moving Picture Co, (C/R) Ken Paterson/Still Moving Picture Co, (B/R) S.J.Taylor/Still Moving Picture Co;11 (C) S.J.Taylor/Still Moving Picture Co, (T/L)Skyscan;13 (B/L) Libby Withnall; (B/R) Macduff Everton/Corbis; 18 (B/R)Ian Britton, 20 (C/L) Glasgow Museums; 21 (B/L) Glasgow School of Art, (T/C); 23 (T/R) Falkirk Museum, (C/R) The National Wallace Monument; 25 (B/L) Angus Tourist Board, (B/R) D.C.Thomson & Co.Ltd; 27 (B/L) Glenfiddich Distillery; 28 (C/L) Caithness Glass Ltd., (C/R) West Highland Museum; 31 (B/L) Harris Tweed Assoc.; 32 all by Richard Welsby; 34 (C/R) British Petroleum Co., (B/L) Just Shetland, (T/L) Richard Welsby; 35 (B) Shetland Times;(C/R) Kevin Schafer/Corbis.

Every effort has been made to trace and credit all images used and the publishers apologise if any have been omitted.

All other photographs from MKP Archives.